Tadpole Books are published by Jump!, 5357 Penn Avenue South, Minneapolis, MN 55419, www.jumplibrary.com

Copyright ©2024 Jump. International copyright reserved in all countries. No part of this book may be reproduced in any form without written permission from the publisher.

Editor: Jenna Gleisner **Designer:** Emma Almgren-Bersie **Translator:** Annette Granat

Photo Credits: Tracy Starr/Shutterstock, cover, 2ml, 6–7; Eric Isselee/Shutterstock, 1; Ondrej Prosicky/Shutterstock, 2tl, 2br, 12–13, 16bl; Ogphoto/iStock, 2tr, 8–9; artiste9999/iStock, 2mr, 4–5; GlobalP/iStock, 2bl, 10–11; tracielouise/iStock, 3; Zeng Wei Jun/Shutterstock, 14–15; jsdeoliv/iStock, 16tl; naturelovephotography/Shutterstock, 16tr; KAMONRAT/Shutterstock, 16br.

Library of Congress Cataloging-in-Publication Data
Names: Nilsen, Genevieve, author.
Title: Los loros / por Genevieve Nilsen.
Other titles: Parrots. Spanish
Description: Minneapolis MN: Jump!, Inc., (2024)
Series: Mis primeros libros de animales | Includes index.
Audience: Ages 3–6
Identifiers: LCCN 2023000286 (print)
LCCN 2023000287 (ebook)
ISBN 9798885248686 (hardcover)
ISBN 9798885248693 (paperback)
ISBN 9798885248709 (ebook)
Subjects: LCSH: Parrots—Juvenile literature.
Classification: LCC QL696.P7 N5618 2023 (print)
LCC QL696.P7 (ebook)
DDC 598.7/1—dc23/eng/20230117
LC record available at https://lccn.loc.gov/2023000286
LC ebook record available at https://lccn.loc.gov/2023000287

Table of Contents

What Is Canoeing? 4
Getting Started Canoeing 8
Canoeing Gear 14
Canoeing Safety 18
Glossary 22
To Learn More 23
Index 24

What is Canoeing?

Canoeing is a fun activity. People travel in small, light boats called canoes.

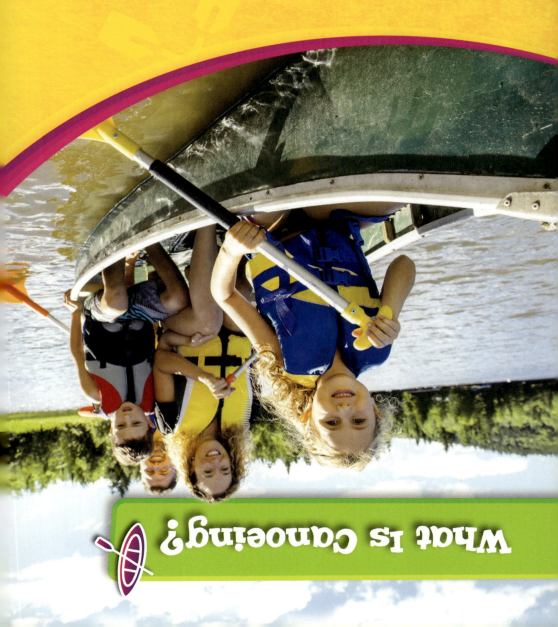

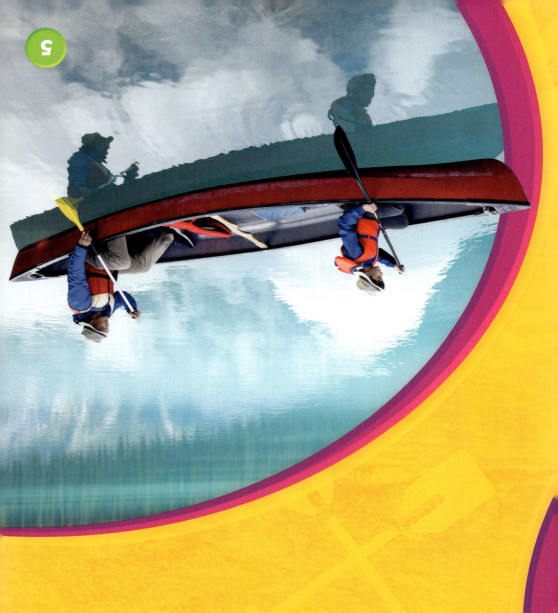

Canoes have pointed ends. They **glide** through water.

People go canoeing on lakes, rivers, and oceans. Some use canoes for fishing or hunting.

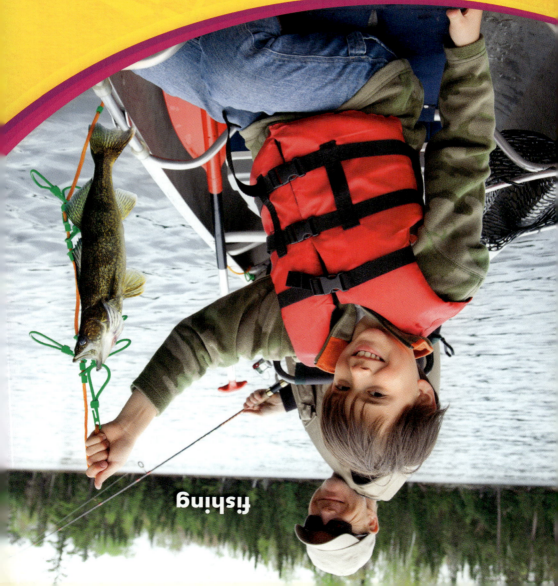

fishing

Favorite Canoeing Spot

Boundary Waters Canoe Area Wilderness (BWCAW), Minnesota

Claim to Fame

- more than 1,200 miles (1,931 kilometers) of canoe routes

Canoeists can ride **rapids** or waterfalls. They enjoy going fast!

Getting Started Canoeing

Most canoes hold two people. To get in safely, one person holds the boat. The other climbs into the **bow**. Then the first person climbs into the **stern**.

stern

Canoeists use **paddles** on opposite sides of a canoe. They push front to back for a forward **stroke**.

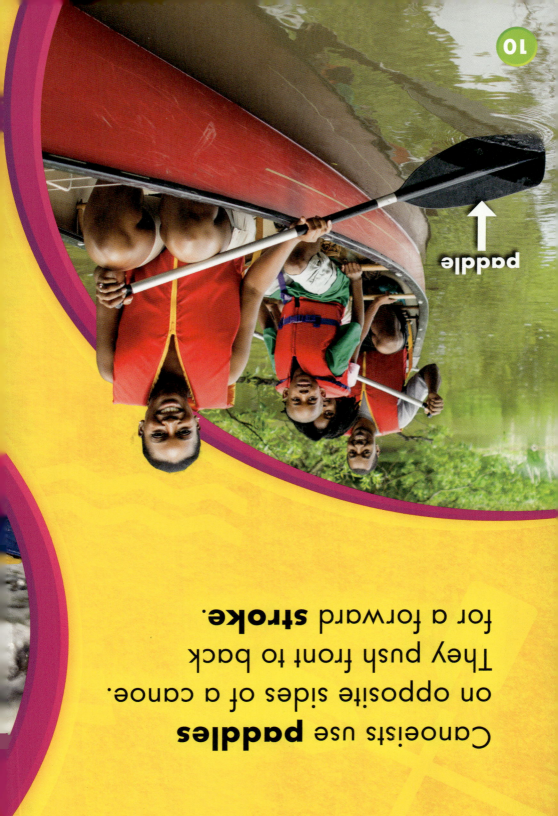

paddle

They push back to front for a back stroke.

The person in the stern steers. They pull water toward the canoe in a **draw** stroke.

Types of Strokes

A **pry** stroke pushes water away. These strokes turn the canoe.

pry stroke

draw stroke

back stroke

forward stroke

Canoeing Gear

Good canoe paddles are light. An extra paddle is helpful if one goes **overboard**.

Cushions make canoeing more comfortable.

← cushion

15

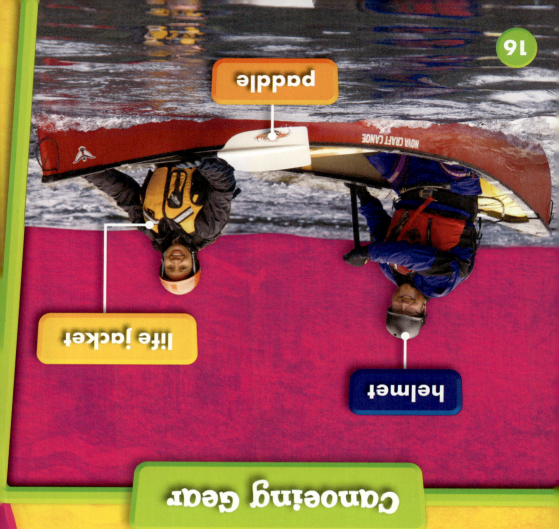

Canoeing Gear

- paddle
- life jacket
- helmet

All canoeists need a life jacket! Bright colors are easiest to see.

Canoeists should dress for the weather. A helmet may be needed in rough water.

helmet

It is best to go canoeing with an adult. Beginners should stay near shore.

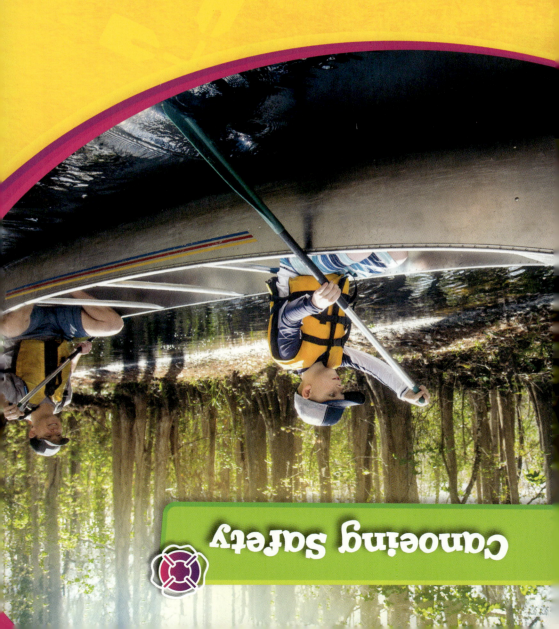

Canoeing Safety

life jacket

Canoeists must wear life jackets at all times.

Canoeists must stay seated. They should sit in the middle. Leaning too far to one side can make a canoe tip.

Canoeing should be safe and fun!

Glossary

bow—the front of a boat

draw—a paddle stroke that pulls water toward a boat to make a turn

glide—to move smoothly

overboard—over the side of a boat

paddles—tools used to move and steer small boats

pry—a paddle stroke that pushes water away from a boat to make a turn

rapids—rough, fast-moving parts of a river

stern—the back of a boat

stroke—a paddle movement that moves a boat

To Learn More

AT THE LIBRARY

Mansfield, Nicole A. *Go Canoeing!* North Mankato, Minn.: Capstone Press, 2023.

Owens, John. *One Summer Up North.* Minneapolis, Minn.: University of Minnesota Press, 2020.

Owings, Lisa. *Kayaking.* Minneapolis, Minn.: Bellwether Media, 2023.

ON THE WEB

FACTSURFER

Factsurfer.com gives you a safe, fun way to find more information.

1. Go to www.factsurfer.com.
2. Enter "canoeing" into the search box and click Q.
3. Select your book cover to see a list of related content.

Index

adult, 18
boats, 4, 8
bow, 8, 9
canoeists, 7, 10, 16, 17, 19, 20
canoes, 4, 5, 6, 8, 10, 12, 13, 14, 20
cushions, 14
favorite spot, 7
fishing, 6
gear, 16
helmet, 17
hunting, 6
lakes, 6
life jacket, 16, 19
oceans, 6
paddles, 10, 14
rapids, 7
rivers, 6
safety, 8, 18, 19, 20, 21
shore, 18
steers, 12
stern, 8, 12
strokes, 10, 11, 12, 13
water, 5, 12, 13, 17
waterfalls, 7

The images in this book are reproduced through the courtesy of: Copyright Crezalyn Nerona Uratsuji/ Getty Images, front cover; marekuliasz, p. 3; Lopolo, pp. 4-5; Romania Lee, p. 5; Willard, pp. 6-7; Wildnerdpix, p. 7; kali9, p. 8; Tom Merton, pp. 8-9; FatCamera, p. 10; LesPalenik, pp. 10-11, 16-17; Elena Eliseeva, pp. 12-13; dolishock, p. 13 (forward stroke); Hero Images Inc./ Alamy, p. 13 (back stroke); Brian Lasenby, p. 13 (draw stroke), -esPalenik, p. 13 (pry stroke); Onfokus, p. 14; Ariel Skelly/ Getty Images, pp. 14-15; All Canada Photos/ Alamy, p. 16; Brocreative, pp. 18-19; nullplus/ Getty, p. 20; Larry Williams & Associates/ Getty, pp. 20-21; Max Topchii, p. 22.